Raena Shirali

GILT

YESYES BOOKS

COVER ART: GION 2015 © YAMINI NAYAR
COURTESY OF THE ARTIST, JHAVERI CONTEMPORARY, AND THOMAS ERBEN GALLERY
COVER & INTERIOR DESIGN: ALBAN FISCHER

FIRST EDITION, 2017
ISBN 978-1-936919-41-3

PRINTED IN THE UNITED STATES OF AMERICA

PUBLISHED BY YESYES BOOKS
1614 NE ALBERTA ST
PORTLAND, OR 97211
YESYESBOOKS.COM

KMA SULLIVAN, PUBLISHER
JILL KOLONGOWSKI, MANAGING EDITOR
STEVIE EDWARDS, SENIOR EDITOR, BOOK DEVELOPMENT
ALBAN FISCHER, GRAPHIC DESIGNER
BEYZA OZER, DEPUTY DIRECTOR OF SOCIAL MEDIA
AMBER RAMBHAROSE, CREATIVE DIRECTOR OF SOCIAL MEDIA
PHILLIP B. WILLIAMS, COEDITOR IN CHIEF, *VINYL*
MARK DERKS, FICTION EDITOR, *VINYL*
JOANN BALINGIT, ASSISTANT EDITOR
MARY CATHERINE CURLEY, ASSISTANT EDITOR
JOHNNA C. GURGEL, ASSISTANT EDITOR, PUBLICITY
COLE HILDEBRAND, ASSISTANT EDITOR
CARLY SCHWEPPE, ASSISTANT EDITOR, *VINYL*
HARI ZIYAD, ASSISTANT EDITOR, *VINYL*

for survival. for your multitudes.

◄ **Contents**

I

her trunk unwinds in an *s*,
red satin saddle & parasol hitched
        to her back. she harbors the groom

        under a gilt dome & faces forward, unendingly
gray. aunties in their finest silks dance
        around her feet, steer her toward

        the bride. i hate to admit i am part of this
crowd, marveling at the girth of her legs,
        thinking: if just one elephant charged

        we'd call it *stampede*. not that she or i
wish death on anyone. the groom
        descends. & she has seen fellow bulls—

        their tusks chipping like bark or shorn at the base.
she knows some things are not meant to be
        taken. i know what will happen to the promises

        we girls make. we say we'll never leave
the herd, but the ceremony will end with a party
where they flaunt their dates while i smoke

        a cigarette where the elephant once stood. for now
we loosen our grip on each other's hands, clap
        wildly, our bangles chiming against

the rhythm, singing along with our broken tongues,
squinting to see the bride through all of this glare,
all of this gold.

Always eat your potatoes. Which is to say, cook
continuously. Stain your fingernails yellow with turmeric
and sample your daal often. No one wants a skinny bride.
Never accept an engagement before you've been with a man
for two years or more. This we will not allow. Don't laugh,
Betee, listen: they will forget your small thicket of mistakes
as long as you remain quiet. Composed. Hide tattoos,
piercings, scars. Grow your hair. Remove the paint
from your toenails. Black polish looks tacky at temple.
Throw out your boots in favor of chappals. Stop drinking
men's liquor. Switch to wine: a glass or two
with dinner, before bed. Which brings us back
to food. Leave a window open when making batata vadas
or bhel puris, or he will leave you smelling of onion
and shame. Wear a sari on fasting days. Always
be tucking in folds. Nobody wants an unraveling woman.

I.

The bride could be anyone decked in crimson: jeweled, gold
chain draped from nose to temple, connected
by piercings—signs that purity can still

sink in. Her henna cracks from wrinkles or wear. Girlfriends
in the audience dab at their eyes. Less important
is the man the spectacle is for. Blossoms line the thin bones

of her forearms, braceleting at the elbow, her slim
bicep cupped by an armband. Fifty-three bobby pins hold
her three-foot fake braid in place (so it stiffens,

not swooshes, not swoons) as she shuffles around the fire.
Her toes, painted for the occasion, tap the carpet
quietly as he feeds her sweets.

II.

In the clouded lens, decked out in beads & a necklace
lined with shot glasses, her eyelids close over with lace.
The night blurs. She sings to herself

at the bar, thinking no one can hear the song
she wants the moment to be. Strobe lights flash her eyes
open. She stares: the mirrored ceiling, her inverted

reflection crowded in by glitter, by trapezoids of light
cast down. Her friends dance slowly though the beat
begs rhythm. One girl's head on the other girl's shoulder.

One girl's hand on the other girl's back.

The season brings a maze of garlands—
jasmine & rose at each threshold. Payals
tinkle through the hallways.
My mother says I look wedding-ready
in a fuchsia sari, my hands a smatter of mehndi
          & borrowed rings.

She tells me
the bride's henna is always the darkest;
each palm a chakra, the prana dimming
delicate fingertips
into sable paisleys. My own peacocked fingers
smell faintly of sandal & lemon.

          With every inch of snow
that falls back in the States,
I'm losing hue. Russet highlights
wane fair. My epidermis sheds
          & sheds. Already, my mother

is scrutinizing the noses
of young men at the reception—scanning,
she smirks. In two weeks, New Year's
fireworks will burst & startle

the muggy Carolina night, but here
cows will munch on plastic
outside the wire-topped wall
around my family's compound.
The streets won't overflow

with the delirious joy
of a kiss at twelve
or a foil-topped bottle's pop.
        My mother will pour me
white wine she smuggled
into her own parents' house,
& ask if I feel buzzed,
or how I liked the bride's
shade of lipstick, & I will answer
the way women are expected to:
                    smile, nod, sip.

i grow up smelling of papaya & coconut oil, my shoulders thin & darkening out—
from bronze to henna on splintered docks, beach towel like a doily
under the caramel sweet of me. i learn from girls with strawberry gloss. they say
fucking is as simple as lemon juice in their hair: that lightening, that lower back lift
& sailing mind. i'm not sad, but the boys who are looking for sad girls always find me.
i don't taste like honey, but the boys want me to melt for them, want my skin
all milk & pearl. they holler from rusted johnboats, hirsute chests smeared with oil. look
how they writhe when i flash a dark nipple. i'm durga, i'm kali, i'm the strange ochre
notch on their bedposts. i'm the spice they didn't expect—cinnamon
powdered over their lips—

As a noun, it's a word that makes most girls I know cringe.
A word whose synonyms—*motion, flux, current*—
remind me of the Cooper, the Ashley, the steady, continuous rivers
I swam in at sixteen, the first time I ever
wore a bikini. I wonder if those girls
think of a body of water—or just of bodies, of boys
who poke fun at *cycles*. It gets tricky for me
with the verb. As in to go along with a series of actions
you may not feel totally comfortable with. To move
in a steady, continuous stream toward or away from a certain
vanishing point of action. As in a lover saying "go with the flow"
was sort of his approach to relationships. I have gone with the flow
all the way up to the moment when time
slows & you see the thing you love
being taken from you. Resistance to the flow is often met
with an impression of me as steady, as in *going steady*, or *why
are you so uptight?* I went with the flow once
at a party in college & the next day threw away all
of my tank tops, every strappy thing
I could find. *Flow* can also refer to blood
between legs, to menstrual cycles, to any kind
of wound & what comes from it. As in no blood was spilled
when he stung my cheek but I felt something *flow*
out of me—steady, continuous. I felt it as I bolted
home, & again when I burrowed into piles of laundry.
We say a poem does or does not *flow*, that things either move forward

or not at all; fish are carried with the river down or upstream;
there's this liquid motion that's steady, continuous,
predictable. Something that cannot be stopped.

In the stampede at Godhra, the first child is trampled.
The Sabarmati Express stalls at the platform

like a suitcase bursting. The bogie's coupling is cut,

the railcar isolated, sprinkled with kerosene.
Look what happens. When we collide

a struck match drops. Our arms flail

from shattered windows. Charred chappals
graze the rails. Dusty pant legs flutter, brimmed

with flames. Our mouths gasp small choking

o's. Now the whole city smells like paan,
a gritty red splatter on gravel-strewn sidewalk.

We know we are too many. When the burnt bodies

are swathed in faded salwars, tossed in the bed
of a rusted pickup, and carried to the Ganga,

we want only the warm silt of flour dusted over

a chapatti. We turn the fan on high, cup a tea light
in our hands. Watch our prayer flicker.

all i remember is rushing water—
the creeks fed into us
as we wetted each other's mouths

with brine. everyone i knew was sixteen
& drunk. nights, we smashed bottles
on ruined civil war forts. damp tights stuck

to our thighs. the city kept on sinking
or swimming, despite the tremors.
each day, new shakes: brick rattler,

wrecking force, familiar thief. we sprayed
fuck the confederacy on the coast's rubble.
after living below sea level for so long
what else could we do?

our smoke rings turned to mist
against the palms. we were driftwood,
tidewrack, abandoned dunnage—

always two shots deep & three feet under.
when the skyline sank, we didn't stop it.
the sidewalk kept splitting open
to let the sea back in.

& abandoned the jellyfish on the beach.
no messages were etched in the sand—
no lovers or children

dragging twigs through the grains.
we were left with cargo ships
rounding the harbor,

left standing amidst a plume of the dead,
sunlight stinting off bodies
the color of melting glass. i admit

it was sunset. i looked at them
to keep from looking at you.
some withered

from tentacle-up,
those trailings purpling
black, manubrium collapsed,

nerve net flinching
like a touch-me-not. you didn't answer
when i asked *which of us*

is more poisonous.
some had lost their luminosity & lay
transparently mauled,

the mesoglea's edges frayed
& milky white,
the whole gelatinous mass

disfigured, less umbrella-shaped
than a shriveling flower
at half-wilt. slowly we inched

close, toed them with sandy shoes.
watched them shudder in response,
wobble back to stillness. look

how i can describe a dying thing
without once saying your name.

SARI
instead of the white gown i will
not wear out of fear or respect
for a god with cerulean blue skin
who looms over david's bridal,
eyeing lace / satin buttons

                    DAWN
                    we sleep in, don't watch mist
                    deluge the dunes / our shadows follow us
                    away from each other, expectedly :
                    the darker one is mine

SEQUINS
skin tight whether on sari or dress
i prefer black : color most
slimming, least fitting
for any kind of bride

                    COINS
                    half-inch thick, i hold
                    under knobbed tongue / no religion
                    has told me to do this

                    i know i am not lucky / in love
                    the elders say it shows

on my too-rough
palms : the tarnish

SHADOW
glitter specks a clad eye
he likes his women
to shimmer / he says
he likes me to shimmer

RING
the elders say i look ready
for it

i have improved :
to improve,
to gain, to lose—to prosper,
above all, in sickness

CHAIN
he knew i was a sure bet / & he was right
i take each link
into my mouth

HOLOGRAM LAMÉ
when he looks at me
in the light i am a different color
entirely

LEAF

i am my own tableau :

madonna, portrait of a loverless

bride, two fingers raised, no kind

of halo or hand blessing my forehead

> *o mere sona re sona re sona re /* to be gilded
> for the fall
>
> *o mere sona re sona re sona re so—*

We lined spent ash on hot black shingles—
                rows of damage we'd bought into. From up there,
        an out-of-focus expanse: wilting marsh, muddy runoff

behind the old swing set. A far off
                kicked ball's echo sounded close.
        The moon hung out in the bleach-blue sky

& we had to make a thing of it.
                I posed for T's camera
        with a bottle in my mouth. Slip-feel of streaked

gloss on warm glass. Her hand on my thigh
                to steady herself. We knew the feeling:
        wanted it: uselessness: limp knees

unshackled from our brains. Cicadas & gnats
                chirruped a chorus of *sleep*
        & *bite*, & we, too, offered up

all the Southern noise we could muster.
                T was unhurried howls & khaki shorts,
        no cottonmouth kick, & me, I was decelerate:

                I was a long *y'all* in the mouth of a pond

Lover & i watch it come in
wisps / clouds like stretching
fingers over the low-roofed houses
the lapsing coast / slow roll arrival then
river birch rubble / everything
bends to keep from rain as the tide
goes up & up—
                    it is noon
            the T.V. static rages its small war

            all my pet names
    have gone missing

▾ ▾ ▾

even the wind off its axis
                ascent, ascent
Lover has left our place
& me without a doorknob watching this
slew of rainbands elongated
out in the distance between this
house & that / between
sand crystals rising like
something is calling
them away from here

▾ ▾ ▾

if we are to measure it by size
& intensity / rotation / air billowing
friction / flood twists around / what isn't
                                        Lover
                    would say it takes two
one warm one / nonchalant someone /
who doesn't mind travelling
up the coast / alone / you see
cool air sinks & calms / the center / where
beneath there is an undertow
a sea / flaying itself in its own wake

The way your apartment windows got that lens flare effect
in early spring. The way umbrellas vomit, turn inside out,

wires screaming for relief. The way on Sunday mornings
your bed was hot with hangover & cold with whiskey stones.

The way I thought of wedding gowns
instead of saris, of bangs & protruding collarbones

instead of bindis & maroon dupattas. The way your face
strained, sweated on a ten speed. The way I forgot India—

wrinkled relatives & garbage trucks with "Horn! Ok. Please"
painted bright red on their front bumpers.

The way you grabbed the fat just under my belly button
& told me to lose weight. The way my mother

scowled under our chandelier, told me to eat
my potatoes—*did I not want my potatoes*

do I ever eat I'm skin & bones & no
I cannot have another drink. The way I ran up the walkway

over the river, intentioned, unintentioned. The way
I gasped for air & then: black. The way I don't remember

walking ten blocks & bent stop signs & puddles of puke.
The way I woke up looking at the ceiling of an ambulance.

The way a cigarette, loyal, still laid tucked
behind my ear. The way the attending nurse said, "Someday

everything gets better." The way your voicemail greeting said
you'd get back to me soon. The way it stormed

all summer. The way I drank rainwater with the pills,
gagged down PediaSure, became a turbid mirror. The way

I made myself stop singing. The way loving you felt
like swallowing gold.

II

◄ **daayan summoning magic**

"This is how everyone in India is brought up—listening to ghost stories." —Sushil Sharma, The Washington Post

if i mandala the room's debris into spirals, paisleys—if i paint
the walls with a simple dye : water & ground fruit—if i scatter her ashes

into my milk, watch them sift their way down
slowly through liquid—if the rain comes when i slide my fingers

into the thick cocktail—back to signs—if the mud on my hands
looks like a chakra—if the sky strips, the crops bow their bald heads—if her body

were granted autopsy, autonomy—if at our core we weren't all
red, red, red—if i chant her name under a thatched roof—if i burn

the roof, see what gets taken with it—if the men ever stop
coming for us—if i tear at a mango with my teeth

under thicker shelter—if i ask the flower to grow & only the sun
pretends to listen—if bloom, if altar, if incense—back

to burning—if i light the sari on the clothesline—if there are many
saris hung hem to hem—if they cradle the flame as they pass it : hem to hem—

if she hadn't struck the match—if the men passed the hut : silent,
darkened from the inside—if the sign for burning weren't always a flame—

light eyes & snake-charmer's
smile. that's what sells out here.
fifteen years i've lived

in corduroy pants
my cācī passed down.
she said, *they're big*

enough to hide the curves.
sure, she was wrong,
but i'm out here begging

all the same. nobody
pinches my ass or yells
kutti when i knock

on rickshaw windshields,
gently tap the black tarp
between me & paying

customer. nobody
wants to bloody my
name—yaar, nobody

cares. i spit in the pock-
marked dirt, let sweat
bead up on my neck, hide

the pulse of growth
in my chest. if there's one
thing i know, it's to clutch

my eyelashes between
two fingers & rip—it's
to never scream loud

enough that someone hears.
it's holding amma's ashes
in my closed fist in the warm

river, then opening it,
watching the gray cloud
get sucked away by a swirl

of muddy water. it's
the palm leftover
underneath: empty,

calloused, the nails
arching into crescents,
just beginning to take shape.

i even thought its name rolled, careened. i thought *bhut jolokia: rough skin, i've had my share.* like the night a white boy bit down on my lower lip, held my hands in place & let my screaming get swallowed with my own blood. let me explain: i crave the saltiest foods. citrus bite, pepper sting. i pour hot sauce onto my tongue, wake with taste buds singed off, the strange ashen afterbirth of numbness growing in my mouth. when he bit through the skin on my chin he left marks. someone else's teeth made evident under my own so my smile resembled a painted skull's—waves of burgundy bruise, waves of grooved wound. & it was cruel not just because i needed no reminder of the scars a boy can leave. it was cruel because i have this history with lovers: snaggletooth on the bottom row, baby tooth stuck behind an incisor. i have run my fingers over jagged men with light skin & come out raw. i know what it means to tongue a napkin after for days. & i had touched his skin willingly, had touched him willingly, had held myself up to the heat, felt its scarlet, its seed, my tongue pulsing underneath, moving but unable to feel itself move

is to turn twenty-four with an ass that refuses
to fit squarely into a string bikini. to miss
america is to miss the point
of each perky, each taut muscle
rippling its way across a wheat field. or to miss
the wheat entirely. it is almost an art: paring

a strawberry into symmetrical slices
for a midnight snack in front of the late night
show. amazing how static can fill
the mind, the gut. o america, i, too, have a stash
of sashes, folded up & boxed, their ribbons too thin
now for my frame. you don't have

to tell me: this body is nothing
like yours—spindly tower
that knows its saunter, knows its shake. you strut
down a lit aisle & miss the brush of grass
against your knees. god, you're as smooth
as they make 'em—teeth vaselined

like a slip'n slide, you are oil & bronze
& glow. miss america, i, too, know
about thigh gaps. i know what goes missing,
the space between girl and grown.
you miss dining room tables, fruit
of your labor, warmth in your belly, warmth

in your home. i am with you: dried flowers
in my hand, the metallic sky
dulling your tiara. look at this mud
where a meadow used to be.

but i threw out our full length mirror. the ads all said expansion shames, so i bought sweats,
   empire waists, shapeless
tunics—the works. you see, we're clearly not lucid anymore, what with the taking
   solace in vertical stripes,
playing *shut off the optic nerve* every time we glance a cosmo cover. each day
   more of us is here,
cocooning us from waif to voluptuous bitch goddess. we're a balloon slowly inflating
   past the confines
of *shimmy*, of *spare*. remember when we were chiffonade-sparse,
   a thimble in a crowd
of bowls? they told us *fit in*, & we took it literally—those days
   all the pills sang *nausea*,
sang *portions*. we were smell-satisfied, anthomanic, content without content.
   i know hunger
is inconceivable & defies arithmetic, but i read somewhere that numbers
   push mush into shape.
we should brush up on our math, bone up on subtraction. go put on
   our smallest dress
& lay motionless in bed while i count us down: two, zero, double—

i'm eating myself. my happy stick figure
stands in the funnel of a meat grinder, waiting
to be cranked into little tubes like play dough
or beef. the part of me that is happy is the part of me

that is dull. but the version that eats is manic:
mouth open under the hole-plate, jaw dislocated
to fit in all the me i want to ruin. my ex-lover
has written in blue at the bottom of the page:

YOU DON'T EVEN KNOW ME.
            now i'm perplexed. who doesn't know
whom? let's try something different: say
we are both in the image, he & i.

say he's cranking that machine & i'm a bony body
with a parenthetical grin. say his irises are black & wide
& looking up at what he will devour. say i can feel
my feet, the twiggy metatarsals splintering

before he swallows them whole. say my little frame
thinks, *this is how it's supposed to be.* say
when the neck of me reaches the gears,
their cut teeth churning, i begin to have doubts

after "Iago's Mirror," Fred Wilson, 2009

       two coal lilies stare back at my eyes
from the atramentous lens. in this mirror

i'm a writhing silhouette: kohl on my lids,
the floral frame petrified, lacquer coating

everything. lacquer as close to black
as blues can get. look

at my legs in the mirror. once, a man held a razor
delicately above. he said, *don't move.* like he'd be gentle

with my calves, the jagged *L*'s of my knees.
       the room was black & my back

curved on hardwood. i felt a prick when he cut
my thigh. this is the bloom

dark outlining can make. he made
no apology. he made his way up   & up.

       look at my lips in the mirror. i mean my mouth,
not the low-down heat i let take over

even though he was a man holding a small weapon
& i was naked   naked

& the lights were out. so many people want *flower*
to mean *pudendum*. or vice versa. either way

the thing can be plucked or shaved & when he finishes
it is stunned: a bright bulb

                        unfurled

◀ **sweet ocean,**

now is not the time to be crooning. you keep upheaving,
leaving rubble in your wake / you make wreckage
of our bones. a building is just a thing / with a skeleton
that doesn't want to hold. you know the orbit
gravity makes of us / holding on to Lover, long
lost, i spin & spin 'til i am my own
hydrofuge / rid me of your creatures, their
corpses. must you render bodies paler
than when they entered / must you bloat us
past recognition / you are the mouth we feed
with all of our shame / toss the flaming picture
into the wave / watch the ashes fall off
of themselves / can i die yet / can i die

light shakes into the cobwebs woven over
all the empty doorframes. when a nearby car's
bass is a feigned serenade
& the moon seems like a dirty thing. passing
fuselage & hospital lights glint & i'm turned on
thinking they flash for me. me, whose favorite window
features a view that's mostly ground. me,
who's quiet, swaddled, blanket-borne
in the fucking eve, waiting on a call
from my only lover, or a friend six states away.
the space between
saying how much i miss everyone i know
& pressing my forehead to my knee
is usually smaller than i think.
the closest body of water
calls itself a river, but it's stagnant.
i call myself a lot to give, but
that's an exaggeration. walking the bank
i trace ripples—lamp-lit contours that fade
into murk. i am two breaths away from saying
i don't understand happiness
when the voice on the other end of the line
asks if it's okay
to hang up now. what is the opposite
of blank noise? insert that excess
here. i want to live off it.

in something sinking, you refuse the hand extended,
   choosing your own skin—bister,

blistered, bitter from such wear, torn
   of your own clawing volition.

shredded dupattas are draped over the parts of you
   where a river would be if you hadn't

gone dry, rent or wrecked the space between your ribs
   too often or liberally. i'm talking

about your tits. or do i mean your heart: the small
   stretches of fabric you cling to as though

you could ever be covered again. you think
   gold anklets charming, a riverbed bell, but

there is no omen strong enough to ward off rust: just
   look at the back of your neck. just look

at the moon not wanting to sync with your cycle.
   married to your terra-firma, you're terra-cotta,

a cracked-up façade snake tracks zag down
   to too-round curves: look at the beast

you're becoming, pulling yourself in two
        directions, one with each hand. on the one,

turmeric, a chakra. on the other, just this. just your skin
        not changing hue. just your body, the same color & tone
                as the mud surrounding it.

I.

the village men fear my evil mouth: so-called *daayan*
feeding on cattle, stirring dust to stifle crops.
i am single. have no man to stand
his two feet on top of my ground & reassure:

                              i am no danger.

me with the lotus painted on her bedroom wall. me the *she-devi*,
        cast lower

                & lower, until i end   in dirt.

II.

men cry for help. daayans, they say, have different
eyes. they say our mantras shrill up the dry air. some forget

they, too, are sudras,   all told   to serve
all bent   to till   all bent   toward ground.

III.

they say we crave the blood of chickens, the piss
& shit of men. they cram it

down
our throats.

IV.

the ohja is always a man. he can sense a daayan's floral
spirit—a wicked thing—in the sal trees, before he brands her

name onto its branches. he waits for inevitable
wither. he performs his white magic. his
purification. tosses rice at white ants. asks that they gravitate
      to nonexistent black.

      v.
they bring me a burnt rooster's ashes, wrapped in banana leaf, sprinkled
with boiled rice. they crouch behind shrubbery waiting.
there is gold   in my house. there is gold   on my hands.

the ohja has his men, his summoning. let them
bribe me. they will break my teeth. they will rape my sisters.
they want it all white—but me, i'm this dark woman. i've been working

their fields under their sun. they come into my
altar, my whitewashed walls. they see me
sitting cross-legged on packed mud
surrounded by figurines of my gods
               & i am shining

                    like a goddamn devil.

his hood flares out, spectacle pattern
like tessellations, the glint of him gilded just so

in the light. the cobra is a garland—no, the cobra
is a man's knuckles, a girl's hair clumped
between them, & you

are the girl. you hold your sadness
with both hands & know
how to drive a shovel between your body
& venom, know the heft

of the handle, splintering your palm.
this isn't your first time.

you killed the last one as he came
toward you, zigzagging, his tracks in the sand
like a graph or table

showing how many more women died
alone this year, in your village
this year, as babies this year, walked
toward him thinking *spectacle*—

& his snake-blood made the sand blacken,
made it curdle, almost, made your blood

curdle, to hear the slicing, to feel his neck
shorn by the blade, & you stared as blood worked
its way back out of his body, thought

of the man who watched you bleed
on his bed the first time & didn't offer
to help. the cobra veers right & you lift the shovel,
pewter almost humming, almost alive,

the blade trembling as you wait
for the snake to change its course—

Palash, flame of the forest, unfurls
against morning: a signal as it begins.
If only to forget the women

we won't speak of, we toss
powder colored with spring crops
& watch our bodies eviscerate
the concentrated tone. If only to celebrate,

we look, for a day, past
the fire our kin have lit—blaze that chases
young women into alleys, or out

of this nation. If only to watch these bodies—only
ours. The town squares, the raised platforms
might have never been—

We could let the full moon & delicacies
fill us. We could trade
turmeric for bits of leaves, fungible entities
ground in marvelous clay pots bursting
with saturates—

& not think of her hair:
Stygian, oiled, gripped or   ripped
by a thirteen-year-old boy. & then
by many boys as young as any of our sons.

If only blue hibiscus & not the hue
of her skin: color she turned at heat-sick

dawn. If only beetroot to decorate,
to complement the rare
green fleck of her eyes. The amla fruit pigment
flings out from my palms.

If only I could tuck a jacaranda
flower behind her ear, place dried tea leaves
in her hands, ask that she color her flesh

back again. I hold the girl's absence
as though I could see her

nails stained red. I hear a woman chasing
her sister say, *Run all you want, I'll catch you,*
hear her sister shriek, hear the crowd—
that mass—   shriek.

                Someone hurls the color of flames
up, like a call to god.

A man approaches me, a blurred eddy
of tones. He mesmerizes. He wields
a fist full of saffron dye.

III

It was dawn, & we went to work
the way we always do—backs curved,

arms swaying over the acid river,
dragging the men's pale yellow dhotis

through the murk. *Om, shanthi shanthi shanthi*
we crooned to the kids on the bank

as the sun made itself felt. That's when
we heard it. Quiet, like a long scream trapped

under a layer of glass. Behind us
the mob entered Nellie

from three sides. Like sheepherders.
Like sheep, children ran from them

to where we stood. To drown away. But
there were boats, too. And men, always.

Men with guns. Men who only want
& want. They jumped from their rafts,

splashed in with spears, & we waded
toward them, knowing the best way

to make a mark is to accept with open arms.

Knowing no one would pay what this cost.

From my tucked-knee coil I hear the news:
        women are interviewed concerning kidnapping

& forgiveness, a girl hacks off her father's head
        with a kitchen knife after a weekend

in his room, a young woman is found
        with her intestines ripped out—raped

with a crowbar—I cannot listen anymore. I sleep
        & dream of a hovering woman—eyes split

down the lid, mouth wrenched open
        as if she is screaming. She floats all night,

sometimes in the periphery, sometimes
        in focus. Up close, her mouth is almost

my mouth. Welts on her skin glow like new. When I wake
        I'm not looking at anything. Once, a lover

called me many words that began with "S"
        & now all my poems are about sheets.

Mold settles in the penned parts of me.
        I grow deep into the mattress, root

my eyes to the pillow. I want my limbs plumbic & my heart
  muttering, I want to be wine-sullied

in the moonwrecked morning, I count my brain cells
  as they spark & fizzle, yes, I want someone

to cleave out my memories, take anything involving
  contusions or his hands or their hands & make room

for the long hours of static
  I am going to put in their place

like all things at that age, it was because of a boy / & i was impaired
in more ways than one. he lounged on a porch hammock / crowded party /
swilling everclear & the girl with her legs strewn over his lap was thinner
than me / taller too / & i had been there first / for years / & he had

slipped his class ring onto my finger & said it was a pre-pre-proposal / but
there she was / twin curls of their lips' corners / he thumbed the edge
of her romper—this is the bane of my memory: that feeling

before the feeling when your insides say *fuck it*
& head up your throat / almost like the feeling when his knuckles

made a red split of my cheek / splotchy vision / before the blackout.
afterward, when i came to / i had held the blonde loom of his head
in my hands, which i remembered when i didn't confront him
when his mouth opened onto hers. i remembered

i am not a strong woman / i prefer floating
to friction / & when i walked, alone, up the onramp,
i was swimming in purple—textured sweeps / spasm

of black on the shore. o, reader, it takes nothing at all for me to shut
down / for my eyes to roll back / cancel / i am so easily excitable / around me
the nightbeds turned violet / the river was a pillow & i wanted to float
through its silvery current / the water ebbed

away from the light & when i slumped against the white
railing instead i was already deep inside a dream
in which there was no party / no fist / no boy's ring on a silver chain

around my neck / only the hush / hush of water
both inside me & out

dare i the greenery flashing by hallucinatory out the window,

parents in the front seat yelling back at me

for wearing a hollister skirt, for cursing

in front of a group of younger indian boys. do i dare

my salwar-clad grandmother at middle school PTA meetings. do i dare

parents, their skin dark around the eyes, darker than some of the other kids' parents—

mom hands me salt scrub & a loofah, says, *get to work.* dare i work

on my tan, skin without sunscreen, dare i explain to a friend

the back of my neck, dare i explain that i am not a "nigger."

dare i use the word. dare i understand *i should not be using this word.*

my friend shakes her dirty blonde hair back & forth slowly:

ain't a difference. dare i know if you put the word "sand" before,

she's right; my people apparently live surrounded by sand, never mind the river,

the himalayas, never mind dharavi & the mountains of sheet metal

& laundry my dad says he once was assigned to during his residency.

says it was electrical & no plumbing & would you look at that,

not a grain of sand in sight. how can i argue

with a question like that—how can i answer *will you have an arranged marriage*

when i'm thirteen—how justify—how rectify—how peel off

epidermis & then dermis & then how rid oneself of a name:

i don all the popped collars, all the pink crop tops,

by God, whom i now presumably believe in, i will show my tits

to the neighborhood boys so they shut up about the sand, so they stop

chasing me down in their pickup trucks yelling *run, nigger run* until i turn

to face & correct them: *SAND-nigger.* dare i sit on the roof of a brick house

with white girls & laugh when they laugh at that story. dare i

coat my eyes in black. dare i chameleon. dare i write. dare i girl.

Watching *Friends* because my mother once forbade it, I am on the phone listening
to a woman unchanged. She says, *uh, yeah, of course we didn't let you watch that,*
like I've grown up to be the kind of twenty-five-year-old who dates around & hates the idea
of marriage. Insert laugh track here. I can only hope my mother means
she wouldn't want me watching a show where all the characters
aren't brown, where not a single one knows *henna* and *mehndi*
mean the same thing, where men come in & out of bedrooms
like small phantoms during the day. Men are always leaving
my room without taking or leaving anything. It would be such stupid
poetry to call them phantoms. Phoebe asks why no one has ever considered
that human existence might be too big for us to fathom. My mother
doesn't want to talk about this right now. Rachel has sex
with her ex in a dentist chair. I have sex with my ex
more places than I can count, & we both feel like shit
the next day, & I feel like shit even now, even here. What did I miss
having not seen these mishaps? Ross confesses he has loved Rachel since ninth grade
& that same year I held my own breasts in my hands and wondered
who will ever want these? I am so lost in this episode.
God, I tell my roommate, *this is F.O.B. as shit of me,* & I'm right,
aren't I, my brown body swaddled in my own charso, my mother
alone while states away my father teaches whole stadiums how the heart works,
both of us staring into tungsten screens, wishing anything had taught us
how to live in this moment.

we row out together. you with a splintered oar, me with my thumbs
between my thighs, pushing on two bruises among many. buzzards perch in packs
above us, thick black bodies in the branches. they rustle & shift
& i am uneasy. these trees, like me, can tolerate a flood. i want to say
it's uncanny how they root underwater, ask, *how can they live in murk like that?*
you row with ferocity & the sun makes right angles of the bald cypress. the water
is black & the bruises on my legs & arms are yellow-tinged. on the shore
plants with pitfall traps lure insects in, their phytotelmata calm with waiting. a fly lands
on a honey gland, slips, disappears. you pull my hot pink flask out from your work boot
& swig. i think every branch in the water is an alligator
& you're not amused by this. a sparrow flits from root to partly-submerged root, ends up
on the bank. you slap the flat of the oar on the water to make waves. you're trying to prove
we won't sink, that the rowboat's chipping teal paint
& perforated hull are nothing to fret over,
but i know in this swamp the plants' cells are lunate, meaning what is caught
cannot escape, meaning the pitchers will drown the smallest bird
& let its flailing body dissolve

barnacles stud my knees as i sink deeper
into pluff mud, free of the ache i once harbored:

the boy who called himself mine briefly, & then didn't
call me anything at all. scattered liquor bottle caps dull

in the sun. their gold foil curls around me.
tide lowers & lowers, & the sun is sick of playing

this pink tinged peek-a-boo with my corpse. the creek bed
is tender with me now i've been here so long. listen:

what they're saying is true. i did this to myself.
not even the palms defend me. but it could be worse.

the oyster bed makes me a pillow, & on the bank
teenagers pass an amber bottle back & forth, back

& forth. the view must be all green ripples, slow-rolling
clouds purple with the weight of rain. they're just

kids. they toss pebbles over my mud spit form. they kill
time, kissing each other's hands. they wait for higher tide.

looking through a telescope at the moon the day neil armstrong died

we locate apollo's landing site on a map that shows
there are two sides to everything
& one is always dark, *maria*,

unfathomable ocean. the dome above is cracked
& only a sliver of seven o'clock sky peeks
down. how dizzying: these fickle attempts

to track my lover's swells, swift black shifts
like a night sky peeling. we are determined
to find armstrong's footing—

all expectation & no satisfaction; all wax,
no wane. & yes we drift in cycles
i don't keep track of anymore.

on the wooden viewing platform
the observatory employee tells me the moon
in this lens is reversed, so i see

east where i should see waning curve.
even if things were right side up
our wrongs don't follow laws

or adhere to astronomy. in the end
nothing negates, & what is bright is too much here.
i cannot find the grounding crater.

the selenic overwhelms
& i clutch the eyepiece, a teetering drunk
unsteady even with my heels off, my lover

smiling up at me from the ground.
did you find apollo? he asks
& i think, o, what a tease you are,

moon: a contradiction, a lie of light
& dark. your surface reeking of gunpowder,
your tendency to decompose liquid.

& i am warm, warm, giving, giving, always feeding
into someone else. every boy i've loved was a body

better than me at the ebb; they made me runnel,
dirty trickle. no wonder i am desperate

to erode. on monday i dip into the hollow cave
of a stranger, shallow pools in the dark

& his overzealous tongue lapping
like rock-shore waves. how long will it take

to quit you again? you ocean, you swallowing, you
take me in your vast blue mouth & spit me out

as salt, & i will not complain. twilight refracts
in my lungs, little molecules of you pitch & linger

in my widening rill. once, i learned all rivers
hold parts of each other: smoothed pebble, fish scale,

the extra tooth behind your top row—oyster-jagged
when i run myself over it. let this mean

what we carry we do not easily leave. let me be
mulled green at your shoreward

bend. let some measure of you settle
with me on the grit fallen bank.

We dangled mason jars from branches: twine, blowpipes bent to hit
their blue glow between the lip's ridges. *I lied to you*, Lover said into the space
between my neck & ear. Pronouns were messy then. Lover spoke
at full volume. There were too many of us in the field
setting tea lights in thick tumblers, blowing kisses at each other like we knew
what it meant. Someone said, *wax easily, always, spills.* The someone was a tall boy
holding a safe in the crook of his arm, against his hip. I wondered what wax could hide
& why—in insoluble red could I put the frail thing that is a heart.
In tawny could I put the girls Lover said were *also that November.* November, now,
could it be where I put a bucket of hot wax in the place of my liver.
My liver can sit in a mason jar counting burn marks on branches, waiting
for winter to end. It is either cooled wax ripping hair from skin or a scar
to keep. A scar for someone else to see & say, *beautiful*, or for Lover to run
waxy fingers over in the center of the field—

Prickle fenced, gridded, the trees
living out here are all frond & pomp,
baring themselves so. Salt wind
whips its song through the dunes.

They must be second guessing by now,
feeling that being naked
is perhaps not freeing, & is, in fact,
cold, especially in open air. I know

that palms are malleable things. Think
like a sponge. The Carolina palm
has been uprooted, shipped across the harbor,
where it has become part of a marooned,

pulpous group. Like a sponge
it takes & takes what punches
are thrown. Does not fissure. Cannonballs
fling their tar-heavy consecration

at a fort made of the ecru trunks. It has taken
me years to say I am not any kind of tree
& I have known for some time:
                    I have to leave you.

rainy days recall other
        rainy days with their dark
                smell—my moon, standing behind me

in the mirror. the sand i now
        resent—snake tracks leading
                away. this must be

the anticlimax. i wait for things
        to let up. i wait so long the ocean
                becomes its own festooning

violence. mist shifts & shimmies
        over a dim creek bed. everything looks blue
                & the christmas song that matches

plays from a beat-up stereo.
        you'll be doing alright with your memories of light—but
                look: here is my body becoming

an island. here is my body
        becoming itself.

So I was wrong about the way bait works: me
with the engine stalled out, waiting for something
to ripple. Long yellow lights off the shoreline.
Fish won't bite if the worm looks dead. If you beat

the thing to death. It was like this before I fell
out of love, too. Me alone with my boots
in the wet sand thinking about prophecy.
Everything smelled a bit rotten, like after a storm,

worms drowning up from the ground.
Let me start over: it was like this
hook on which I was thrashing but not
dead just yet. So maybe I was the one in love

with a worm—dangling from barb, it gleamed.
It thrashed & thrashed & slowed to a coil.
Was I gracious enough to let go? The cold beach,
the shoreline: every parallel route told me this

would go on forever. They might have been wrong.
It has been evening a long time. Misty. Before the fish,
the bite. Before, it was a bright dead day.

IV

We stood by quietly as the mosque fell. Or was pulled.
The celebration turned riot & all the idols
lay decapitated at Nirmal Nagar. The elephant

god without an elephant head. Even without
the cold, we shivered. The buses around
us enshrined in flames. Who could tell

which temple was falling, and when? Of course
we were in Jogeshwari when we found them.
The sickles. Iron rods flaking dark red chips

into the dirt. The Constable face down
in the garbage. Seventy-two times
we intervened. Seventy-two times we killed

& were killed. Standing over us, the attackers
mocked. *Where's your army now,* they said,
& we did not have an answer.

ARE YOU A WOMAN FOR SOCIETY?

from a billboard advertising masala chai, downtown Mumbai

AKA: when sipping chai on a muggy day, do you:

      A. dab your upper lip with linen

                or

      B. curse your cācī, from whom you inherit
            your tendency to sweat it, to provide
            four different kinds of sugar so a guest
            never feels out of place?

it may be that your husband, who works for the rails
(not on them) does not care much for your particular
blend. or it's your saas—dimpled hips falling over the top
of her petticoat. her weight frightens you, so you have acquired
a taste for liquid, tannins of every sort, assam, monsoons,
their ability to fill, to drown.

AKA: when brewing your husband's family's recipe do you:

      A. crush the star anise with a pestle, careful to leave
            no rust-colored point unground

                or

      B. cut corners, use the allspice when saas isn't looking,
            accept your role as bahu-from-america, smirk
            when saas & husband like the western version
            better?

you probably enjoy your first cup of the day alone,
very early, before light fails to filter through
the perpetual overcast that means more
rain, always. a mosquito buzzes next to your ear
& all morning you swat it, collecting bites, scratching
at the ghost-shaped swellings, cursing it for never
alighting quite when you expect

We're by the window chopping mung beans when the glass
shatters outside—we duck at the thud
when the taxi ceases to leap. The air smells of coast

& trash & burning cabbage. Smoke & firelight
make ginger of the sky. Fire like we've seen before. This
is our cue. We crawl to the bed, flatten

our bodies underneath. Warm linoleum
presses our cheeks. Our sweating hands
touch while detonations refract

down the block. We stay like this overnight—toes
alert, eyelids twitching. The television susurrates
of ladders pouring from the hotel's holes, hostages

by the hundreds, the tick of explosives
into gutting. We recite our parents'
phone numbers, secret questions for bank accounts,

things we've hidden in the bottoms of drawers. We apologize
for what we've each written about the other
in emails, journals. Nine men are shot in the hotel lobby.

As the newscaster's voice wavers in the fading
moonlight, we whisper of hidden gold jewelry.
We make such brave promises.

In the corner, men tied together
off white sheets, ochre curtains. They threw open windows
to shimmy out. I considered speed, organization.
How my body would fail me if my weight were in its hands.
Things on the sixth floor were brightening. The heat
felt like that day in late September when the endless
puddles suddenly dry. No matter the season. This city hummed
through the night, somehow calculated in its mayhem.
Mayhem meant my hands working quickly to untie
the tightly wound ropes. Mayhem was bodies face down
on plush rugs, young boys' faces cast in tungsten glow
as they made their demands. I wanted to cradle their cheeks
in my palms, say, *Go outside. Enjoy your life. Leave behind*
whatever got you into this. I didn't know I was already begging.
Mayhem is not knowing whether to run or blindly
pull a trigger. It's a planless, painless thing. It has no idea
when the night will end.

Because you were walking hand in hand.

> *rough, calloused palm*
> *he helps his grandmother*
> *sing ghazals by night:*
> *thrums a tabla, hums*
> *a swar, closes his eyes*
> *when her voice chimes in*

Because he was from another village.

> *he wears a white button up*
> *dusted with streets*
> *i don't know by name*
>
> *we stop*
> *at a corner mart*
> *buy sodas*
>
> *we drink*
> *from separate straws*

The things we have seen
our women become.

> *a gentleman, he*
> *says he'll walk me home*

> *he kisses my forehead*
> *under the simple leaves*

You were spotted in public
under an Alstonia:

> devil tree.

> *men whose faces i have known*
> *for years*

> *men swarm, lash, beat*

We know when a gesture calls
for blood.

> *a little bit of his heart*
> *was beating in the road*

We know what we have worked for.

> *my family sings*
> *the mourning song*
> *before there's anything*
> *to mourn*

Some of us chant, our children
listening, catching on.

> *i know enough*
> *people yelling*

sounds like one
long scream

Some of us don't say a word.

i shut my eyes

Nothing more can be said about concrete
than the cold. A lightless filament, bulb dancing

on shredded wire, is the only thing

shining on me now. The moon's nerve
is pinched outside the barred window

crooning its redemptive song—

No, here the moon is a coroner
guarding each fortuitous grave.

Yes. I didn't try

to ignore the surge. Something
shifted in my lungs & suddenly

collapsed—a botched house,

a flimsy stack of cards. I thought, *this
must be how it feels to drown*

with your mouth open.

I had painted a series: black & white
portraits of my lover's torso

tracing the bends

in blind contour first. Sometimes
when I looked at him I saw a spine

full of stars, like what's best

was always left
elsewhere. That's how it is

with light. It's one thing to travel

& another to wane. This is what
I tell myself: I tell myself

my mantra is not stupid, but

I have this stupid mantra
about freedom & youth

that fails me whenever my lover

is in a funk, smelling of funk.
I have a motto that says nothing

is better than something, right?

Right. I have a mantra that says nothing
is colder than my untouched skin.

                    This summer
our curtains are always pulled shut. When I wake
it's to the sound of metal scraping stone.
Bulldozers tear chunks of brick
from the building next door. You say,

We've lived here too long, & you might be right:
the sheets are slowly stiffening, the headboard creaking
away from the frame. Your hair shakes out sawdust
when you climb on top. Everything we own together
is covered in film—the lint on the radiator, the spit

on my neck, debris outside our windows, grime
in the hall where you've tracked your work back in.
                    This summer,
I live in a plash of various salts from your body. I burrow
despite your leaving. I say, *You smell like dirt*, but mean,

Your teeth are square blessings
when they graze. Tomorrow morning will be
just like this. You will thank my earlobes for liking
the touch. You will thank my elbows for bending
that way. Even though you are leaving

me, this will not be a gesture of solace.
Even on your neck   the scent of pine.

B,

Your father owes me money.

      You are skinny & wear the jeans.

          You owe me explanations.

C,

Love letters should not be signed

with recklessness or paw prints.

      Most Decembers, I want to be with someone

who will grow out his beard.

K,

You should get that small yellow tooth checked out.

Most dentists are pretty good with anesthesia.

Novocain.   Nitrous oxide.   They'll do what it takes.

      Anything to knock you out.

J,

Beard clippings litter the bathroom sink.

I forget which are yours, which are his.

This is not to say

      I had both of you at the same time.

It is to say:

      you all wore the same red plaid shirt.

         It is to say:

            I don't know who I am alone.

S,

You are a dull lamp. Mottled man.

Hand-rolled American Spirits,

farmer's tan swigging an almost empty bottle.

You are sweat knit across brows,

  the last bit of whiskey I swirl around the glass,

  residue melting slowly into itself.

D,

O, what worship is a forehead kiss!

A fella like you oughta know better

  than to commit like that.

W,

Remember when you asked, *Isn't it funny*

what we want out of music?

We were talking about records, probably.

That they are cyclical &.

  My tastes in music have changed.

    I still don't have an answer for you.

M,

You make ex-

cuses & excuses, & won't own up to departure.

& o, let's play that game again,

the one where

  it's comforting

    to me

      knowing

   that it comforts you

    knowing

most nights
I hug a cold pillow.

Knowing no one's
scratch marks
zigzag my back.

On your porch, two vases of tulips
wilt, predictably: cut

stems, petals just amber, water
sucked up & dingy. A dog snores on the lawn.
You have your feet up, a brand of cigarette

you don't usually buy dangling
between trimmed nails. Green crust
under chin where your face mask

avoided the splash. A kid bikes by, yells,
WHORE. He is too young to know

that sting. You bite into a tomato & think
of a meal you made with your last lover—
some kind of curry—& end up

masturbating, supine on porch slats. People
walk by, hardly noticing at first. Your lovers'
old names come out of your mouth
before you can catch them.

You try to picture the last one, but
can't summon his face. A crowd

gathers. Boys sell peanuts, munch
popcorn. They aren't turned on
so much as confused.

You're a full-time circus act. You moan
to the crowd about a finale, but it's overcast
suddenly & your audience has left.
Except one kid

kicking up mulch by the sidewalk.
He looks down at his white sneakers

& reminds you of lemonade. You adjust
your dress & are taking your plate back inside
when he asks, *You don't want*

any dessert? & you think, *No*, but don't
have the words to say why just yet.

I left Lover when I found dirt roads—at a party for another couple,
soirée complete with deer heads lining a fixed-up barn's walls,

absinthe, strung lights. In pairs, we played pissing games—
collect the most Monopoly money, hurry to tie the knot

without a hitch in the line. Gracefully. Fever trees in the distance
waved their unadorned leaflets. Everyone abuzz with talk of the rural setting.

Oh, quaint wedding. Oh, quiet ceremony. Lover called me over to admire
the heads on taupe walls: deer pelt, pliant skin.

We spoke of pre-party waxes, manicures, facials. Judged by fur, or
its lack, we girls—alert to being overheard—looked down, giggled

into plastic cups of chardonnay. Are we always measured
in terms of smoothness? Pink balloons deflated at leisure.

Lover studied the tanned, mounted hides. Out in the backwoods
I thought stars would flare like an angiogram, that the vast pasture

would daunt at two a.m., that something like fear would crawl out
from the black between trees & force me to stay, but the acres swaddled me

in moonlight: placental, ancient. I wasn't a fragrant bouquet
of anything but a thing without roots to put down in this field

you wake alone & sit in the gray, dank light under a few madly-
spinning blades. damp forehead, damp cheeks. he left you
just months ago & it has been raining since.
outside, umbrellas do a catwalk of black, black,
faded blue. it seems you are always at a wedding
listening to breakup songs in the corner. the bride's gown or sari
shimmers by the light of a rain-soaked moon. but then, there is always
a bride, a body of light to illuminate her cheeks just gorgeously.
you are on the floor, watching the skyscrapers cradle
their separate cranes. they seem to have stopped trying
to reach the silly dome of the sky. so, you & your interminable
hunger: curled up on linoleum—still wet from last night's
muddy heels. you obsess over the crow cawing
through the thin glass like some omen, & dream of a quality of sunshine
that never existed for him, forgetting how all the while rain
hasn't once touched your blessèd head.

The agarbatti plumes its familiar signal: peace, sandalwood, fire alarms
shut off. Ganpatis, as always, line my shelves: coal, red, golden. They seem level
with me now. They aren't like other gods, don't demand
change. I turn on every bulb, burn each wick. I know what you're thinking. Lonely
is a word for it. My mother sings me prayers through a dimly glowing screen,
& I try to match the lyrics. Outside, palms sway
with the thick Southern breeze. The incense wanes. I burn
through three matches trying to get it right. Slowly
I find the Gayatri Mantra, chant under my breath. I'm this bright
lit thing, far from the white boys walking by, dressed in their seersucker,
their pale stripes. Past my lawn, the coast threatens to lap itself up. The suburbs
are cast in shadow. My mother asks if I have prasad—any fruit will do—if I'll eat
a laddu & accept the new light this darkness can offer. A truck revs its engine,
sends sooty shearwaters into the night. I find a lychee, bite into it. I say *yes*.

No longer living in any kind of garden—no chipping benches, no dusty petals or body heat, *no respite, no respite*—I make for the bottom. Pellucid ice above seems a lunar dome. I am inside—underneath—this roving planet. Fuck the so-called return to nature: its verdancy, its promise that things will continue to grow. I know the nidus of apathy & settle into steadily flowing frost like microbe onto moon. On other continents, warmth rises, swelters: a girl dances in flashing lights on the last day of the year, her short dress flaring up. Around me black water swirls, forces things to sink. Dark mineral, local mineral, I'm here to burrow, follow the borehole to lake's end. Feeding off those that are most like me, I become another link to remote moons—soar, pitch, shimmer. What more can I do? Yes, the garden was full of miasmic bloom, but what is there to miss of a distant sun? Here, I take what I need from unknowable depth easily, as things do in the dark. I find the newest opacity on record & plunge further into the ice stream

"camouflage" quotes Warsan Shire.

"A Railroad Puja" is for the victims & survivors of the Godhra train burning of February 2002.

"daayan summoning magic" & "black magic" refer to the ongoing practice of witch hunting in some parts of rural India.

"Holi: Equinox Approaches" & "CROWD / GIRL" are for the twenty-year-old woman who was gang raped "on a raised platform in front of her entire village" as "punishment for having a relationship with a Muslim man, who was not part of the community" (*The Independent*).

"Kopili, 8:30am" is for the victims of the Nellie Massacre of 1983, wherein not a single culprit received punishment for the murders of 2,191 victims. Most of the victims were women, children, and seniors.

"The Fort" refers to the use of palm trunks to defend Fort Moultrie in South Carolina.

"The State Para-Military Force Speaks" is for the victims of the Mumbai Riots of December 1992.

"From Our Bedroom" is for the victims of the 2008 attacks on the Taj Mahal Hotel and Oberoi Trident.

"K.R. Revisits Room 623" is set during the 2008 attacks on the Taj Mahal Hotel. The poem is for K.R. Ramamoorthy, who was held hostage while his fellow (younger) hostages escaped using alternate means.

I am beyond grateful to the editors of the following magazines, where the following poems first appeared, often in younger versions:

The Adroit Journal: "monsoon season, one"

Banango Street: "Stasis" & "The Downing" & "to miss america"

Better: Culture & Lit: "say i am a series of creeks"

Blackbird: "the procession"

The Boiler: "camouflage" & "i hate to break it, body" & "the woods"

Boston Review: "The State Para-Military Force Speaks"

Cosmonauts Avenue: "daayan summoning magic"

Crab Orchard Review: "Kopili, 8:30am"

Crazyhorse: "cells:" & "feet planted" & "Fishing With Broken Lure"

Dusie: "DARE I WRITE IT"

Fogged Clarity: "the waves receded in december"

Four Way Review: "looking through a telescope at the moon the day neil armstrong died"

Gulf Coast: "Engagement Party, Georgia"

HEArt Journal: "Adorn"

Muzzle Magazine: "Aubade"

The Nervous Breakdown: "at the peninsula's tipping point"

Ninth Letter: "black magic"

No More Potlucks: "Grit Cycle" & "i know i am in love again when"

Ostrich Review: "black light"

Permafrost: "ghost pepper," "monsoon season, two," & "sweet ocean"

Phantom Limb: "self-portrait after my ex-lover's self-portrait"

Quarterly West: "Holi: Equinox Approaches" & "New Year as an Extremophile"

Sundress Publications' *Political Punch Anthology*: "in which the teenage girl poses as a boy, begs in the street" & "Stasis"

THEThe Poetry Blog: "A Railroad Puja" & "flow" & "lowering"

Tupelo Quarterly: "Diwali: New Moon"

Winter Tangerine: "if i wrap myself in gold" & "Now You Are Eating Alone"

Immeasurable thanks to KMA Sullivan & the YesYes team for giving *GILT* a home, for your editorial brilliance & fearless advocacy.

Thank you to the teachers & mentors I was lucky enough to encounter while writing this book. Thank you Kathy Fagan for teaching me how to be free in verse & spirit; Jennifer Schlueter for your eye, & for your empathy, faith, & time; Emily Rosko, for this path, for helping me travel down it, for ekphrasis & Italy & your continued friendship and guidance. And thank you Aimee Nezhukumatathil, Tarfia Faizullah, Jericho Brown, Brenda Brueggemann, Nickole Brown, Jessica Jacobs, Jamaal May, Brenda Hillman, Timothy Donnelly, Ricardo Maldonado, Claudia Rankine, Juan Felipe Herrera, Rachel Zucker, & Tracy K. Smith. Your generosity bolsters me. Your kindness gives me strength.

Deepest love & eternal gratitude to Megan Peak & Paige Quiñones, my lit witch collective, without whom not a single poem in this book would exist. Thank you for being my voice when I lose my own, my favorite makers of poems, my best friends.

Thank you to the incredible writers, lit lovers, & artists I'm thankful to call my community, including Shelley Wong, Janelle DolRayne, Mikko Harvey, J. Brendan Shaw, Cyrus Hampton, Cait Weiss, David Winter, Rebecca Turkewitz, Lauren Barret, Megan Kerns, Nina Yun, Nathan Thomas, Michael Marberry, Sonnet Gabbard, Taneem Husain, John Slefinger, Lauren Krouse, Hanif Willis-Abdurraqib, Rachel Wiley, Tiffany Salter, Jake Bauer, Daniel O'Brien, Joey Kim, Ayendy Bonifacio, Colleen Kennedy, Jamie Lyn Smith, Hannah Reed, Graham Barnhart, Silas Hansen, Lily Watkins, Nate Fann, Ali Pearl, Nini Berndt, Kristen Simon, Hannah Stephenson, Mel Burkeet, Michael McDevitt, Andrew Luft, Martha Schneider, Tiffany St. John, & so many more.

Thank you Shefali & Girish Shirali for your understanding & support. And thank you, Rohan, for growing with me. SSG forever.

Thank you Kati, my sunshine, my sister. Thank you Mike & Harley, my heart, for making every day possible.

RAENA SHIRALI is the author of *GILT* (YesYes Books, 2017). Her honors include a 2016 Pushcart Prize, the 2016 *Cosmonauts Avenue* Poetry Prize, the 2014 *Gulf Coast* Poetry Prize, & a "Discovery" / *Boston Review* Poetry Prize in 2013. She has also been recognized as a finalist for the 2016 *Tupelo Quarterly* Poetry Prize & a 2014 Ruth Lilly Fellowship. Her poems & reviews have appeared in *Blackbird*, *Ninth Letter*, *Crazyhorse*, *Indiana Review*, *Pleiades*, *Four Way Review*, & elsewhere. She was raised in Charleston, South Carolina, where she recently taught English at College of Charleston, her alma mater. Born in Houston, Texas, the Indian American poet earned her MFA from The Ohio State University. She currently lives in Lewisburg, Pennsylvania, where she is the Spring 2017 Philip Roth Resident at Bucknell University's Stadler Center for Poetry, & serves as a poetry reader for *Muzzle Magazine*.

FULL-LENGTH COLLECTIONS

i be, but i ain't by Aziza Barnes

The Feeder by Jennifer Jackson Berry

Love the Stranger by Jay Deshpande

Blues Triumphant by Jonterri Gadson

North of Order by Nicholas Gulig

Meet Me Here at Dawn by Sophie Klahr

I Don't Mind If You're Feeling Alone by Thomas Patrick Levy

If I Should Say I Have Hope by Lynn Melnick

some planet by jamie mortara

Boyishly by Tanya Olson

Pelican by Emily O'Neill

The Youngest Butcher in Illinois by Robert Ostrom

A New Language for Falling Out of Love by Meghan Privitello

I'm So Fine: A List of Famous Men & What I Had On by Khadijah Queen

American Barricade by Danniel Schoonebeek

The Anatomist by Taryn Schwilling

Panic Attack, USA by Nate Slawson

[insert] boy by Danez Smith

Man vs Sky by Corey Zeller

The Bones of Us by J. Bradley
　　[Art by Adam Scott Mazer]

Frequencies: A Chapbook and Music Anthology, Volume 1
　　[*Speaking American* by Bob Hicok,
　　Lost July by Molly Gaudry
　　& *Burn* by Phillip B. Williams
　　Plus downloadable music files from
　　Sharon Van Etten, Here We Go Magic, and Outlands]

CHAPBOOK COLLECTIONS

VINYL 45S
After by Fatimah Asghar
Inside My Electric City by Caylin Capra-Thomas
Dream with a Glass Chamber by Aricka Foreman
Pepper Girl by Jonterri Gadson
Bad Star by Rebecca Hazelton
Makeshift Cathedral by Peter LaBerge
Still, the Shore by Keith Leonard
Please Don't Leave Me Scarlett Johansson by Thomas Patrick Levy
Juned by Jenn Marie Nunes
A History of Flamboyance by Justin Phillip Reed
No by Ocean Vuong

BLUE NOTE EDITIONS
Beastgirl & Other Origin Myths by Elizabeth Acevedo

COMPANION SERIES
Inadequate Grave by Brandon Courtney